EMPOWERED
FOR WITNESS, WORKS AND WONDERS

EMPOWERED
FOR WITNESS, WORKS AND WONDERS

For foreign and subsidiary rights, contact the author.

ISBN: 9781950718337   1 2 3 4 5 6 7 8 9 10

Printed in the United States of America

TABLE OF CONTENTS

EMPOWERED FOR WITNESS, WORKS, AND WONDERS

Billy Wilson

In April 1906, as a physical earthquake was occurring in San Francisco, a spiritual earthquake was happening in Los Angeles. The ensuing Azusa revival launched the Pentecostal/Charismatic renewal around the world. What began as a handful of people now encompasses more than 600 million Spirit-filled believers around the world. What caused this wind of the Spirit to spread so rapidly? Is it possible to personally experience that same supernatural empowerment to share the gospel of Jesus Christ, demonstrate the works of God, and experience signs and wonders?

The Holy Spirit is the effectual person of the Trinity—He executes the desire and plan of the Godhead. He is a doer, and we know Him mostly by what He does. The activity of the Spirit was present in the Genesis creation account. As the Word was spoken by the Father, the wind of the Spirit was breathing, or hovering, over the earth. Thousands of years later, Jesus' departing words to His disciples promised transformational power for witness when the Holy Spirit came upon them.

After the once-fearful Peter powerfully witnessed of the life-giving Messiah, Jesus Christ, thousands were converted to The Way. Immediately, the newly formed church began to exhibit the wonderful works of God. By the end of Acts chapter 2, the church was supplying the needs of the poor, caring for widows, adopting slaves, reaching out to the young, lifting up the oppressed, and responding to natural crises. In addition, people brought their sick and those tormented by evil spirits and all of them were healed (Acts 5:12, 15–16).

Embracing the gift of the Holy Spirit will not only give you dynamic words for witness, but will release within you the creative, life-giving agent of empowerment for service. Your life as usual will be radically transformed as God begins to open doors for the performance of signs and wonders through you.

WHAT IS THE HOLY SPIRIT SAYING TO ME?

_____

_____

_____

_____

_____

_____

ACTIVATION

- Reflect for a few moments on the awesome, creative power of God through the Holy Spirit and thank Him that this same power can operate in your life.
- Witnessing is simply sharing what you have experienced in your life. When was the last time you witnessed to someone about the transforming power of the Holy Spirit you have received?
- Make a personal commitment to Christ to share the Good News with one individual this week.

WHEN THE SPIRIT FALLS

Samuel Rodriguez

In a world full of moral relativism, cultural decadence, spiritual apathy and ecclesiastical lukewarmness, there exists good news; The Holy Spirit of God still moves. He continues to convict. He continues to reveal Jesus and he continues to sanctify.

When God's Spirit descends, everything changes.

When the Spirit fell, Joseph stood recognized and came out of his pit. So Pharaoh asked them, "Can we find anyone like this man, one in whom is the Spirit of God?"

When the Spirit fell, Moses encouraged the prophetic.
When the Spirit fell, the Israelites listened to Joshua–enabling him to conquer.
When the Spirit fell, Saul became a different person.

Correspondingly, when the Holy Spirit comes upon you, he empowers you to come out of the pit. When the Spirit falls, you prophesy. When the Spirit falls, you conquer your promise and when the Spirit falls, you will be changed into a different person!

Yet there's more! When the Spirit fell, David was anointed to reign.
When the Spirit fell, Gideon blew the trumpet and won the war.
When the Spirit fell, Samson broke the ropes that bound him!

Get ready, for as the Spirit falls upon you in this season, you will function under your anointing, you will win the battle and the all the things that held you back will be broken.

Accordingly it's time to rise up. Arise with the power of His Spirit and. . .Walk like Enoch, Believe like Abraham, Dress like Joseph, Stretch like Moses, Shout like Joshua, Dance like David, Fight like Gideon, Pray like Daniel, Build like Nehemiah . . .And live like Jesus!

For it is not by might nor by power but my Spirit says the Lord!

WHAT IS THE HOLY SPIRIT SAYING TO ME?

_____

_____

_____

_____

_____

_____

ACTIVATION
- Pray for the Holy Spirit to fall upon you!
- Ask the Holy Spirit to empower you to be a different person.
- Pray that the power of God's Spirit will bring favor upon your life, work, and ministry.

OPEN TO RECEIVE

Robert Morris

"But you shall receive power when the Holy Spirit
has come upon you; and you shall be witnesses to
Me in Jerusalem, and in all Judea and Samaria,
and to the end of the earth."
Acts 1:8 NKJV

Have you ever received really bad news, and yet you some-how sensed an unbelievable peace and knew everything was going to be okay? That was the Holy Spirit working in your life. When you don't have enough faith on your own, the Holy Spirit gives you the faith you need to make it through. He empowers you and gives you peace. You just have to be open to receive His help.

The only way you can receive His help is by spending time in prayer. Prayer alone prepares you to hear the Holy Spirit and receive His gifts. The more time you spend in prayer, the more clearly you are able to hear His voice and the less often you mistake it for your own.

The Holy Spirit continually intervenes miraculously in our lives, but we often think it's mere coincidence. The reality is the Holy Spirit not only wants to do miracles *in* your life, He also wants to do miracles *through* your life. Nothing is too hard for the Holy Spirit. He wants to empower *you* on a dai-ly basis. The Holy Spirit is everywhere, and His gifts are for every believer—including you! Are you open to receive His gifts and His help today?

WHAT IS THE HOLY SPIRIT SAYING TO ME?

_____

_____

_____

_____

_____

_____

ACTIVATION

- Seek the Lord every day, listen for His voice and be transformed by His Holy Spirit.
- When you have a decision to make, take the time to ask God for His will in the situation.
- When you're praying, don't do all the talking. Be still and allow the Holy Spirit to talk to you.
- Ask the Holy Spirit to direct and redirect your prayer life so that you are constantly in relationship with Him.
- The Holy Spirit wants to give you faith to believe for certain things that you've been praying for. Receive that faith today! Don't doubt and don't talk yourself out of it!

FURTHER STUDY

Romans 8:26–27; Galatians 4:6; James 5:13–18; John 14:12; John 16:7; Psalm 55:16–17; Jeremiah 29:12–13; Psalm 51:1–3

WHAT ACTS TEACHES ABOUT OUR EXPERIENCE OF THE HOLY SPIRIT

George O. Wood

The Book of Acts teaches four things about our experience of the Spirit—what the Spirit is doing when He comes upon us. First, the Holy Spirit creates unity among us without producing uniformity. When the Spirit of God enters us, we do not become clones. In fact, the Scriptures say that the Spirit places great variety in the Body of Christ—varieties of ministry, personality, ministerial office—all flowing out of the one Spirit. The Spirit ministers to us the life of Jesus, which is the source of our unity, but He also brings us to Christlikeness without making us "cookies" cut in the exact same shape.

Second, the Spirit taps the potential in our life that no one or nothing else can reach. No one's life is ever the same after having encountered the Holy Spirit. No person in the New Testament would have ever realized the potential in his life unless the Holy Spirit had been upon him. No matter what our talents and personalities are, and no matter how much energy we bring to any particular assignment or task, only the Holy Spirit can touch the depths of potential in our lives and draw it forth for the Kingdom of God.

Third, the Spirit is always leading us in two dimensions simultaneously. He's always leading us deeper into God and He's always leading us out into the world. The Spirit's desire is to make us more spiritual, more Godly, more like Jesus. He wants to lead us deeper into God. At the same time, the Spirit leads us out into the world, because God loves the world. The Father gave His Son to save the world. Jesus told us to go into the world, but He said we cannot go unless the Spirit comes upon us. He told the disciples to wait for the Spirit.

Fourth, the Holy Spirit is indeed a Person and as such, you can resist Him, ignore Him or welcome Him. He waits to be received; He waits to be invited. Jesus said to ask the Father and He will give you the Holy Spirit. The Spirit will not storm down the door of your life. He seeks an invitation. We must ask, seek and knock and welcome the Spirit.

WHAT IS THE HOLY SPIRIT SAYING TO ME?

_____

_____

_____

_____

_____

_____

ACTIVATION

- Spend time thanking God for the creativity of His Spirit. Thank God for your own unique gifts, talents and abilities that have come from Him.
- Pray for the fulfillment of all the potential and promise God has spoken over your life.
- Set an example for other believers by the way you welcome the Holy Spirit into your daily life.

ROLE OF THE HOLY SPIRIT

Margaret Court

"'Out of his heart will flow rivers of living water.'
But this he spoke concerning the Spirit."
John 7:38–39 NKJV

John's Gospel gives us Jesus' explanation of the role of the Holy Spirit on this earth. The Holy Spirit is to lead, guide, inspire and empower the Church of Jesus Christ.

According to Zechariah 12:10, the Holy Spirit is a Spirit of grace and supplication. He will teach us what we need to know, guide us into all truth, show us things to come and glorify Jesus. He is called the Paraclete, our Comforter, Helper, Intercessor, Advocate, Strengthener and Standby. He will always bring glory to Jesus and point you to His Word.

John 16:14 says that the Spirit will reveal, or transmit, the things of God to us. Sometimes transmission of power or knowledge can even come to us when we are unaware. We can be in a faith–filled environment and not necessarily "feel" anything; however, the Holy Spirit transmits power, or healing, or revelation in and by His Spirit, and we suddenly realize that we have grown or been given revelation.

The Holy Spirit helps us to pray and anoints us to pray. We don't necessarily need to bring a list to prayer—we need to learn to yield to the promptings of the Spirit and begin to flow with Him. As we wait on the leading of the Holy Spirit, prayer will never be boring!

WHAT IS THE HOLY SPIRIT SAYING TO ME?

_____

_____

_____

_____

_____

_____

ACTIVATION

- Choose your favorite of the Holy Spirit's names and meditate on it. Write down ways He has revealed Himself to you.
- Ask the Holy Spirit to anoint you with a fresh anointing as you pray today. Practice yielding your thoughts and speech to His promptings and try to flow with Him in a new way.
- Let go of any personal inhibitions that are restricting the flow of His living water in your life.

FURTHER STUDY

John 14:16, 26; John 6:13–16; Ezekiel 11:19; Romans 8:26; I John 2:20; Romans 7:6

SPIRIT-EMPOWERED PRAYER FOR THE LOST

Rob Hoskins

The critical ministry of God–breathed, Spirit–empowered intercession on behalf of lost humankind has historically been at the forefront of Pentecostal mission. However, I dare say that it is becoming a diminished and less recognizable activity in the Church both here in the US and increasingly around the world. Paul says in Colossians 1:28–29, in what I consider his life's mission statement, "Him we proclaim, warning everyone and teaching everyone with all wisdom, that we may present everyone mature in Christ. For this I toil, struggling with all his energy that he powerfully works within me." The Greek word for "struggle" here is *agónizomai*—I agonize, but not alone; it is His Spirit working in me. Paul avows that he has power to "strive" in the Spirit for those without Christ, but only as Christ works in him and by him.

Sometimes in our independent, self-realizing culture we overestimate our abilities and grossly underestimate the Spirit. I fear in the midst of our narcissistic faith—our therapeutic religion—that we've forgotten what our primary mission is. The work of evangelism and the victory of seeing the lost come to Christ are primarily won in deep intercession and Spirit-empowered prayer. My tendency is to want to go to battle with Joshua in the field, but I'm learning that the intercessors on the hill—Moses, Aaron and Hur—require much more of my time and attention.

WHAT IS THE HOLY SPIRIT SAYING TO ME?

_____

_____

_____

_____

_____

_____

ACTIVATION

- Pray with the Holy Spirit. Pray in tongues and ask for an interpretation so that you can also pray with your understanding.
- Pray for lost people you know who need Jesus in their lives. Pray for their hearts to be softened and their circumstances to point them toward Jesus.
- Pray for the Word of God to be active in the lives of unbelievers. Pray for a release of God's Spirit who will woo many people to His heart.

HOPE AND THE HOLY SPIRIT

Alton Garrison

Faith and hope are similar but distinctly different. In addition to the measure of faith, Romans 10:17 (ESV) declares that faith can grow through the educational process of "hearing, and hearing by the word of Christ." Faith is more educational while hope is more emotional. Faith is related to miracles; hope is more about morale.

Hope is a favorable, confident, happy anticipation of good things to come. Hopeful people are happy, generous, and positive. Hopeless people are negative, bitter, discouraged, and defeated.

Satan's attack is more against our hope than against our faith. It is easier for him to discourage us emotionally than to defeat us Scripturally. Anyone who has experienced loss, sickness, tragedy, or pain will often hear Satan's lie: "If God really loved you, why would He allow that to happen to you?"

When we lose our wealth, we are hindered. When we lose our health, we are handicapped. But when we lose our hope, we are emotionally paralyzed. When we look at our health, finances, relationships, family situations, or joblessness and all looks hopeless, we must not give up.

"May the God of hope fill you with all joy and peace in believing, so that by the power of the Holy Spirit you may abound in hope" (Romans 15:13 ESV).

WHAT IS THE HOLY SPIRIT SAYING TO ME?

_____

_____

_____

_____

_____

_____

ACTIVATION

- Recognize that God is your source of hope.
- Believe you have not lost your faith.
- Write in your journal the emotions destroying your hope. Release those to God and let Him recharge the hope in you.

THE HOLY SPIRIT: BREATH OF GOD

Gordon Robertson

"For in Him we live and move and have our being."
Acts 17:28 NKJV

Back in Genesis, it describes how we were made. *"And the LORD God formed man of the dust of the ground, and breathed into his nostrils the breath of life; and man became a living being"* (Genesis 2:6-7). It is from the breath of God that we actually get our life.

The same thing happens when we are born of the Spirit. When we are reborn, it is from the breath of God. In the Gospel of John, Jesus gives His disciples the Holy Spirit. Just as God breathed on Adam and gave him the breath of life, Jesus breathed on His disciples in John chapter 20: *"'Peace to you! As the Father has sent me, I also send you.' And when He had said this, He breathed on them and said to them, 'Receive the Holy Spirit'"* (John 20:21-22).

Jesus didn't just breathe on the disciples 2,000 years ago. Every time we are baptized in the Holy Spirit, it is God's breath on us. Just imagine that. I think most Christians today believe the baptism in the Holy Spirit is only a one–time event. We see such an event in Acts chapter 2, but we fail to look forward to Acts chapter 4 where they get baptized in the Holy Spirit again. It says very clearly in Acts chapter 4 they were *all* filled with the Holy Spirit when they were in a prayer meeting. This means we can be filled with the Spirit continually.

We don't have to walk around as if there are some moments when we are filled with the Spirit and other moments when we're not. We can be continually filled with His presence. Imagine how that would transform your life! The baptism in the Holy Spirit is not a one–time event; it can be a continuous thing for all who believe.

Christians need to be filled with the Holy Spirit now, more than ever. We need to be filled with His authority and have the power of God working in our lives. We live in perilous times; this is not a time for us to take off the armor of God and go relax. We need to be fully armed and fully prepared with the Holy Spirit.

WHAT IS THE HOLY SPIRIT SAYING TO ME?

_____

_____

_____

_____

_____

ACTIVATION
- Open your heart to the fresh filling of God's breath, His Spirit. Get comfortable with the idea that baptism in the Spirit is not just a one-time event, but a continually needed experience in your life.
- Thank God for His breath of life in you!
- Take time to pray through your spiritual armor and let the Holy Spirit show you strategy for your day.

FURTHER STUDY
Acts 4:31; Ephesians 6:10–19

THE REVEALER OF TRUTH

Lisa Bevere

The Holy Spirit is amazing! As the revealer of all truth, He confirms God's Word within our hearts. This third person of the Trinity who came to indwell us at Pentecost provides the counsel and direction we need to live well before the Father.

When truth is spoken, the Holy Spirit confirms it to you and in you. There is a distinct prompting and a release of life. You will feel a resounding "Yes, listen and receive this" inside of you. You will feel as though light and strength, truth and freedom are being poured out upon you. This will happen even if the message is one that brings correction. You will witness inwardly that it is true and the illumination will bring with it the power to embrace the cleansing, correction, or admonition. This can happen as you read the Word, worship, pray, hear a sermon, or speak with a close friend.

As we approach the celebration of Pentecost, I encourage you to be mindful of the power and presence of the Spirit who lives inside you. Let's heed the whispers of His voice and embrace the truths He discloses in our hearts. Our churches will be full of truth when they are full of the Spirit. As the Church is empowered by the truth, we will extend the life of God to the nations!

WHAT IS THE HOLY SPIRIT SAYING TO ME?

_____

_____

_____

_____

_____

_____

ACTIVATION

- Listen for the Spirit's voice in your heart. Write down what He tells you, and any specific instructions or Scriptures He gives.
- Listen throughout your day for the quiet promptings of the Holy Spirit. Make note of them instead of letting them pass by unheeded.
- At the end of the day, go back and pray through the things the Spirit told you and impressed upon you. Discuss them with Him and find out what else He wants to say

THE POWER OF THE FULLNESS OF THE HOLY SPIRIT

Young Hoon Lee

For a larva just hatched out of an egg, even a little pebble or a small twig seem like great barriers to overcome. However, if the larva will press on through all those "obstacles," it will eventually become a beautiful butterfly which can fly easily over them.

In the same manner, we may meet a variety of obstacles in life that make us despair. So many people are frustrated because they believe they are incapable of overcoming the challenges they face. The reason they do not live a victorious life as a child of God is because they remain a spiritual "larva." Without the fullness of the Holy Spirit, we are powerless, and fall short of all the wonderful promises of God about victorious Christian life. In other words, unless the Holy Spirit transforms us into spiritual "butterflies," we will not be able to overcome life's obstacles by ourselves.

When we receive the fullness of the Holy Spirit, our lives change comprehensively. We will win any battle against sin with the power of the Holy Spirit. We can solve any problem by the help of the Holy Spirit. Best of all, we can have a most intimate relationship with our God. If you want to live this kind of fascinating life, all you need to do is invite the Holy Spirit in and let Him have control. You will then enjoy a life of fullness with the Holy Spirit.

WHAT IS THE HOLY SPIRIT SAYING TO ME?

_____

_____

_____

_____

_____

_____

ACTIVATION

- Identify any places in your spiritual walk where you have been stuck in the "larva" stage. Invite the Holy Spirit into those places and ask Him to transform you into an overcomer.
- Praise the Lord for His overcoming Spirit in you! Give Him thanks for power to rise above despair, depression, negativity and fear. Thank Him for filling you with faith and victory!

SPIRIT OUTPOURED

Jürgen Bühler

If there is one nation on earth which has a Biblical right to receive the outpouring of the Holy Spirit, it is Israel. Many prophets prophesied to the Jewish people throughout history that a day would come when God would pour out His Spirit on Israel. On the day of Pentecost, when Peter stood up to speak to his Jewish brethren, he referred to Joel chapter 2 and declared that "the promise (of the Spirit) is to you and to your children" (Acts 2:39).

The prophet Isaiah also foresaw revival for Israel. As he looked around Jerusalem, he found his people in a state of crisis and devastation. But then he declared that this would only last "until the Spirit is poured upon us from on high" (Is. 32:15). The direct result of the outpouring of God's Spirit is peace, which is exactly what many Jews and Palestinians yearn for today. The true roadmap for peace in the Middle East is the through the outpouring of God's Spirit on both Jews and Arabs.

Today there is a new, dynamic move of the Spirit gaining momentum in the Middle East. According to Operation World, the nation with the highest rate of church growth in the world is Iran, and second to that is the nation of Afghanistan! God is in control. Here in Jerusalem we are hearing about revivals in Algeria and even in Egypt, and we know that God's Word promises one day His Spirit will again be poured out in Jerusalem and on the house of David.

WHAT IS THE HOLY SPIRIT SAYING TO ME?

_____

_____

_____

_____

_____

_____

ACTIVATION

- Pray for the peace of Jerusalem, and pray for the outpouring of the Holy Spirit in Israel to bring revelation of Messiah Jesus.
- Pray for the continued revelation of Jesus Christ to people in the Middle East and that many would receive Him.
- Pray for miracles, signs and wonders that will point people to the one true God and His Son, Jesus Christ.
- Ask God for an outpouring of His Holy Spirit in your home, family, friends, community and beyond.

PREPARING JERUSALEM FOR THEIR KING

Wayne Hilsden

God is looking for people to prepare Jerusalem for the King. I believe the day of the Messiah's return is not far away. The world is experiencing excruciating labor pains, and the time between contractions is lessening. No one knows the day or the hour, but we can feel something in our bones. His return is soon. How can we prepare Jerusalem for the King's return? A look at Psalm 48 provides us with the answer.

1. WITNESS.

Knowing the time is short, we in Jerusalem need to witness while we can. Yeshua communicated the good news using physical things in this city as tangible illustrations—a pool of water, an upper room, an olive garden, a sepulchre. The city of Jerusalem continues to be a treasure house full of illustrations for the Gospel. Everywhere we walk in this city we find conversation pieces that naturally lead to spiritual things. We need to frequently remind Jerusalemites of God's eternal plan of salvation for this city.

2. AUTHENTIC PRAISE AND WORSHIP.

Psalm 48:1 says, "Great is the Lord, and most worthy of praise, in the city of our God." If there's any place in the world where the praises of God should be lifted high, it is in Jerusalem. Our aim is to have worship that springs from the heart, yet is sensitive to the unique character and culture of Jerusalem.

3. PASSIONATE PRAYER.

Jerusalem's security is not her walls and citadels, but her God. Psalm 48:3 says, "He [God] has shown Himself to be her fortress." Verse 8 says, "God makes her secure forever." We have a vital part to play in the peace and prosperity of this city. Psalm 122:6 tells us to "pray for the peace of Jerusalem." The prayers of God's people are what will keep Jerusalem in these precarious days.

Will you commit to pray regularly with us for the peace and salvation of Jerusalem? The Lord speaks to us in Isaiah 62:6–7: "I have posted watchmen on your walls, O Jerusalem; they will never be silent day or night. You who call on the Lord, give yourselves no rest, and give him no rest till he establishes Jerusalem and makes her the praise of the earth."

WHAT IS THE HOLY SPIRIT SAYING TO ME?

_____

_____

_____

_____

_____

_____

ACTIVATION

- Pray for the peace and security of Jerusalem through the power of the Holy Spirit.
- Pray for Jewish hearts to be turned to Messiah Jesus.
- Pray for the Messianic believers in Israel to be bold in sharing the good news of Jesus with their families and friends.

SPIRIT-EMPOWERED PRAYER

Cindy Jacobs

This is one of the most powerful Biblical examples of Spirit-empowered prayer. The disciples who struggled after Christ's resurrection went from weakness to strength in the midst of persecution.

What an example to us for our everyday lives! Life's circumstances may hand us trials, grief, and anxiety, but we are not meant to let these challenges defeat us! Each of us has choices to make. Do we go ahead with what God has given us to do? Will we reach our destiny and purpose in life, or go down in defeat?

The difference between those who succeed in life and those who do not is that one has learned to pray in the Holy Spirit and the other has not. Spirit-empowered people who prosper have learned the art of spending quiet time with God, and by doing so, have learned the art of intercession.

As you read this devotion today, you might be afflicted on every side and undergoing a season of distress. Fear not! God will help you turn those circumstances around. The answers to life's complexities will come to you when you practice Spirit-empowered praying. Trust that God will give you a new boldness as you receive His answers, and new pathways of blessing will open before you.

WHAT IS THE HOLY SPIRIT SAYING TO ME?

_____

_____

_____

_____

_____

_____

ACTIVATION

- Take time to quiet your self before the Lord and pray in the Spirit.
- Stop and listen to the answers that He will give you.
- Search the Scripture for passages that the Holy Spirit will speak to you. Pray those Scriptures under His inspiration.

"WITH"—OR "IN" AND "UPON"

Jack Hayford

Here is a lesson Jesus taught His followers about the Holy Spirit. The Holy Spirit is a resident counselor. The Greek word here is interesting: *parakletos*—"para" (beside), "kletos" (call)—one who is called alongside to help. There isn't a single thing needed in the Christian life that He isn't there to provide. Note the difference in the prepositions that are found in the passages before us today. Jesus said the Spirit was "with" them, but later would be "in" them and "upon" them. I take these prepositions to mean that the Holy Spirit was "with" them prior to Pentecost. Prior to Pentecost their lives lacked character and consistency. They cast out devils, but on other occasions they seemed to be somewhat influenced by them.

Simon Peter is a case in point (Matthew 16:23). The disciples were loud in their assertions of loyalty, and loud in their blunderings and misunderstanding. The Spirit was most certainly "with" them—helping, encouraging, and revealing—but He was most certainly not "in" them or "upon" them. When the Spirit came "in" and "upon" them at a later date, then their fitful living became faithful living, and their erratic loyalty became everlasting loyalty.

Today in the lives of many Christians, the Holy Spirit seems to be working on the outside rather than on the inside. Actually, of course, the Holy Spirit is resident "in" every Christian, but He wants more than just to be resident—He wants also to be president! How is it in your life and experience? Is the Spirit a passing guest or a permanent guest?

WHAT IS THE HOLY SPIRIT SAYING TO ME?

_____

_____

_____

_____

_____

_____

ACTIVATION

- Think about the ways the Holy Spirit comes alongside you to help you.
- Think about what it means to have the Holy Spirit living inside you, and what it means for the Holy Spirit to "come upon" you.
- Thank God for the power and life that He gives you through His Holy Spirit.

WHEN THE HOLY SPIRIT COMES TO STAY

Gordon Moore

When the Holy Spirit comes into our lives, He brings the presence of God. The work of the Holy Spirit within our lives is to connect us with God—to create fellowship, relationship, guidance and fruit.

The Holy Spirit presences Himself in man, but this can present problems for us because He is beyond all human understanding, convention, mentality and opinion. In our self-indulgent, self-oriented and self-pleasing culture, we are not prepared for the unpredictable, miraculous moments of the Holy Spirit!

However, the Holy Spirit is not subject to our personal preferences, convenience, comfort or rights to individual autonomy. When God shows up in your circumstances in a "Holy Spirit moment", you can trust it is His right timing. God interrupted Saul on a very important errand and changed the entire course of his life in that one moment. The Apostle Peter had a Holy Spirit moment when he saw a vision and was convinced to take the good news of Jesus to the Gentiles. Barnabas ended up in the middle of a major move of God at Antioch and helped to raise up Paul, the greatest apostle, after he had his own Holy Spirit moment.

What about you? Do you need a Holy Spirit moment? We all need the Holy Spirit to move on us—to save us, fill us, renew us and change the way we think and live.

WHAT IS THE HOLY SPIRIT SAYING TO ME?

_____

_____

_____

_____

_____

_____

ACTIVATION

- Confess any resistance to the Holy Spirit as you recall times He did not fit into your plans.
- Get back on the same page with Him today—soften your heart to His ways and His timing on things.
- Invite Him into your day and give Him permission to bring a Holy Spirit moment whenever He would like.

DYNAMITE POWER!

Danny de Leon

I was tuned in to the History Channel on TV, watching a program about one of the greatest human feats in history: the building of the Panama Canal. "Wow," I thought, "what would they have done without dynamite?" Maybe the project would have been accomplished, but it would have taken so much more time. I thought of the many access tunnels that have been dug through mountains, blasting holes through bedrock to get to the source of water or oil, removing the side of a mountain to get to gold or diamonds—all with the use of dynamite!

In Acts 1:8 Jesus said, "You shall receive dunamis/dynamite after that the Holy Spirit comes upon you." Why dynamite? Maybe because He knew that the Church would need "dynamite" from time to time: to blast through spiritual mountains of resistance so we could spread the Gospel, to blast through other spiritual structures so the Holy Spirit could flow, or to remove any other kind of obstacle that would try to hold back the blessings of God.

Today, in this world fraught with mountains of resistance, we need divine dynamite more than ever! We need Holy Spirit power to accomplish greater things for God and to get to the untapped resources for His Kingdom work. O God, send us the Power!

WHAT IS THE HOLY SPIRIT SAYING TO ME?

_____

_____

_____

_____

_____

_____

ACTIVATION

- Receive the deposit of Spirit-power God has for you to-day. Open your heart and let him fill you with dynamite that will flatten the works of the enemy!
- Allow the Holy Spirit to lead you in meditating on His wonderful works. Let your mind see what the Spirit is saying. Pray for Spirit–led visions of His power at work in you and through you.
- Locate any blockages in your life where the enemy is resisting God's work, and let the explosive power of the Holy Spirit blow up the blockades! Listen as the Spirit leads you to pray, and say what He is saying.

THE HOLY SPIRIT: OUR FATHER'S GIFT

Stevie Mitchell

I love prizes. I love giving them and I love getting them. For me, it's all about finding the perfect prize—that prize that will tell another how much they are loved and how special they are. The prize says; "I know you. I know what makes you tick. I know what you need, and I know what will make you smile." It is so much fun to give a gift just for the sake of giving. My gift has to say, "I love you! I believe in you! You are fearfully and wonderfully made! You are a masterpiece!

- John 4:10 Jesus replied, "If you only knew the gift God has for you." (NLT)
- John 17:7 "Now, they know that everything I have is a gift from you." (NLT)

Growing up, my daddy encouraged and reinforced my gift giving. I grew up in the 60's & 70's in a small town in Vermont where my dad owned the local drugstore. The store was also the Hallmark store, specialty shoppe, and Christian bookstore—which made gift giving easy. My dad also had a passion for giving gifts and modeled for me. It was common for my dad to open the cash register, hand me money and say without a customer knowing, "While I fill this prescription, go next door to the grocery store and get the family groceries." Or, he would call me to the back of the store and say, "Mr. 'So & So' hasn't thought about buying his wife a birthday present. Go pick out a gift, and wrap it up for him to take home to his wife." He trained me to watch and listen to know what would really bless people.

I can only imagine what was going thru the mind and heart of Jesus that day as he shared with the disciples—the guys that he had spent days and night with for the past three years. He knew what made the disciples smile. He knew the ultimate gift He would give them. A gift that would release them into their destiny. A gift that would give them power. But even more than what would make them smile, Jesus knew what made His Daddy smile. He knew how much his Father loved to give gifts. He knew that Abba had the perfect prize and it would soon be time to give them the gift that would change everything.

Although it would be difficult, it would be a sacrifice that would cost Jesus much. His heart was full of excitement because he too loved to give gifts. His Daddy had taught him well. The cost—Jesus would have to die, rise, and return to his daddy so that the ultimate prize could be given—the Holy Spirit.

The Father knew what we needed! He knew what would make our hearts smile.

WHAT IS THE HOLY SPIRIT SAYING TO ME?

_____

_____

_____

ACTIVATION
- Pray for the Holy Spirit reveal God's gifts to your life.
- Ask the Holy Spirit to empower you to be a gift-giver to others.
- Pray that the power of God's Spirit will anoint your gifts and talents for His greater glory.

ANOINTED TO BE CONQUERORS

Prince Guneratnam

God has empowered you to be an overcomer and a conqueror. No matter what your circumstances may be, they do not need to dictate your future. Because you are a child of God, His anointing on your life breaks every yoke of bondage. The Bible says that you are being changed from glory to glory and from faith to faith. You need merely to believe and do the will of God.

The anointing of the Holy Spirit is the key to being a conqueror because you do not have power on your own. Paul explains, "I do not understand what I do. For what I want to do I do not do, but what I hate I do . . ." (Romans 7:15, 19-20). God has promised you the Holy Spirit who anoints you and gives you the power to turn away from a life of sin, to live righteously for the glory of God and to have authority over Satan.

The New International Version translation of Luke 24:49 says that you have been "clothed with power from on high." The anointing is like a garment that clothes you. A civilian who enlists as a soldier is given a military uniform that authorizes him to do the job. In ancient times, the uniform was like an armor which protected the wearer from the attacks of the enemy. Likewise, the Holy Spirit is given to you for that reason; the Holy Spirit equips you for battle to overcome Satan's temptations and your old, sinful nature.

Therefore, it is important that you be filled with the Holy Spirit. Let the Holy Spirit fill you again and again. When the Holy Spirit comes and touches you, you will not be the same. You can be emancipated, delivered and set free!

WHAT IS THE HOLY SPIRIT SAYING TO ME?

_____

_____

_____

_____

_____

_____

ACTIVATION

- Thank God for filling you with the Holy Spirit. Quiet your mind and heart so you can feel the Holy Spirit's touch.
- Remember times when the Holy Spirit has helped you overcome temptation and trouble in the past, and spend time thanking Him for His work in your life.
- Pray for a fresh anointing to fully become all God created you to be, and to rise up as a conqueror!

SAINTS MINISTER

David Ferguson

Everybody agrees that the church's job is to make disciples, yet we are not sure what it means to be a disciple. Do you have a clear vision of what a true disciple is? Do you know where you are going and how to get there?

The ultimate goal of discipleship is to become like a Person—the unique God-man, Jesus. With this in mind, we find a framework for Spirit-empowered discipleship by focusing on the Holy Spirit and how He brings context and empowerment to our relationship with Jesus.

Jesus was called to love and to serve, and all the way to Calvary He did just that. Some sobering examples from Christ include: "The greatest among you will be your servant" (Matthew 23:11). "I am among you as the one who serves" (Luke 22:27). "Now that I, your Lord and Teacher, have washed your feet, you also should wash one another's feet" (John 13:14).

The words "saints minister" provide significant insight into what it looks like to be a fully devoted and empowered Christ-follower. Paul emphasized this when he said that Christ has appointed some "for the equipping of the saints for the work of ministry [service]" (Ephesians 4:12).

We minister to the Lord, and we also minister His Word to others. When we invest ourselves in ministry to the Lord and experience life-changing moments in His Word, the natural outflow will be the Spirit's empowering grace to share His life and love with others. Can you imagine the possibilities of Spirit-empowered saints ministering to the Lord, and then from that intimacy ministering His Word, His love, His gifts, His grace, and His message of reconciliation to others? That is what a true disciple looks like—the passionate love of Jesus on display to serve, help and bring people to life.

WHAT IS THE HOLY SPIRIT SAYING TO ME?

_____

_____

_____

_____

_____

_____

ACTIVATION

- Take a few moments to meditate on the relational aspect of being a disciple of Christ contrasted with a rational model based on knowledge, or a behavioral model, consisting of a list of do's and don'ts. Do you recognize a need for Holy Spirit discernment more than human development?
- Express your gratitude for the gifts and fruit of the Spirit that empower you to have more than intellectual knowledge of Christ. Ask the Lord to help you establish and maintain an intimate, loving relationship with Him that naturally flows out through ministry to a broken and hurting world around you.

THE AGENDA OF THE SPIRIT

Samuel Rodriguez

We live in a world where people are bound—bound by sin, pornography, sexual immorality, addiction, alcoholism, depression, loneliness, dismay, anxiety, fear, confusion, the past, failure, and defeat. Do you know why so much bondage exists?

The enemy understands that the most dangerous human on the planet is not the one with riches, guns, armies, or fame. The most powerful human on the planet is a person set free by the blood of the Lamb. Why?

Because it was a free man who approached Pharaoh in Egypt and said, "Let my people go." It was a free man who stepped into the Promised Land and declared "As for me and my house, we shall serve the Lord." It was a free man who stared down a giant called Goliath and said, "You come against me with a sword, a spear and a javelin, but I come against you in the Name of the Lord God Almighty." It was free young people who refused to bow and subsequently exhibited freedom even in the midst of a fiery furnace. It was a free man who prayed down fire from heaven and then shouted "Get ready, here comes the rain!" Although they had been held behind the prison bars of human laws, spiritually free disciples replied to their captors, "Which is right in God's eyes: to listen to you, or to him? You be the judges! As for us, we cannot help speaking about what we have seen and heard" (Acts 4:19–20).

The Spirit of Pentecost not only looses the chains of injustice and sets the oppressed free; He breaks the yokes of anxiety, fear, and defeat, empowering God's people to proclaim the message of freedom to others.

WHAT IS THE HOLY SPIRIT SAYING TO ME?

_____

_____

_____

_____

_____

_____

ACTIVATION

- Pray for God's people to cry out to the Holy Spirit in the midst of their bondage. Pray for eyes to be opened and hearts to be healed as believers learn how to walk in freedom
- Appropriate freedom for yourself in any areas you are struggling. Declare your freedom by the blood of the Lamb and the power of the Holy Spirit.

FRUITFUL CHRISTIAN LIVING

George O. Wood

When I was a little boy living in northwest China, we didn't get fresh fruit and vegetables. I loved oranges, though. Somehow, we had gotten an orange and I saved the seeds to plant an orange tree so I could have oranges on a regular basis. I put some dirt in a little clay pot, put the seeds in it, and then put it by the stove. It was bitterly cold, and I knew I had to keep it warm. I really expected that within a few months, I'd have a tree growing out of my potted plant with oranges falling off of it. I'd watch it every day and nothing would happen. I watered it faithfully, but nothing ever grew. I think as Pentecostals we often want things to happen instantly, but the fruit of the Spirit tends to be more developmental. The development of fruit in all of the disciples was a growth process. It did not happen immediately. Peter did not become the rock overnight; it happened over time.

I see the fruit of the Spirit as sequential in development, much like the locks on a canal. A canal operates to move ships into a closed space called a lock. One body of water is lower than the next body of water they're moving to. Gradually, by the ship going uphill or downhill, it moves through a sequence of locks. Each of the locks the ship moves through fills up with water and floats the ship higher. Slowly, it moves into the next lock and goes on. I think developing the fruit of the Spirit is like that. Beginning with love, we progress until we've moved all the way through and come at last to that hardest of all to develop—the fruit of self-control.

The fruit of the Spirit tells us God is far more concerned with who we are than what we're doing. If you're looking for

God's will for your life, don't look first of all at where God wants you to go, or even what God wants you to do. Look first of all at what God wants you to be. Probably ninety-nine percent of knowing the will of God is being the person God wants you to be. Because if you are that person, you can go anywhere and do anything and you'll be guided by God and in His will.

WHAT IS THE HOLY SPIRIT SAYING TO ME?

_____

_____

_____

_____

_____

_____

ACTIVATION

- Pray for the fruit of the Spirit to grow in you. Feed your soul with God's Word and let the Holy Spirit bring His rain to the good soil of your heart.

Think about the fruit that is easily seen in you; think about the fruit that is not yet visible in your life.

Ask God to cause every fruit of the Spirit to grow out of your spiritual walk with Him.

ENCOUNTERING THE SUPERNATURAL

Billy Wilson

Holy Spirit is power.

Both the Old and New Testament words translated "spirit" convey the meaning "breath, wind or blast of air." We may encounter the Holy Spirit like a gentle breeze of comfort and assurance, but we may also experience winds of supernatural power performing signs and wonders. Was miraculous empowerment unique for the early church? Or is it something you can experience today? Are you offering words of blessing and witness and practicing dynamic acts of love and affirmation, but perhaps have forgotten one of the greatest gifts you can share is the hope of supernatural help?

In Acts chapter 3, Peter and John were going to the Temple in Jerusalem for their usual time of prayer when they encountered a man who had been lame for more than forty years. This meant he was a young child when Jesus was born. No doubt, he had been nearby when Jesus healed the blind and the lame in the temple courts. The disciples had passed this prime spot for the beggar—the gate Beautiful—many times on their way to prayer. What made this particular day any different?

These disciples had experienced an encounter with the resurrected Christ. They had heard Him reiterate the Father's promise of Spirit baptism and watched Him ascend into the heavens. More importantly, they had spent time praying and fasting in the Upper Room until they were filled with the promised Holy Spirit. They had stepped out of their usual day-to-day existence into a power-packed life poised for supernatural wonders. Have you positioned yourself for the wind of the Spirit to blow into your life? Are you willing to be a channel for this power to work through you?

WHAT IS THE HOLY SPIRIT SAYING TO ME?

_____

_____

_____

_____

_____

_____

ACTIVATION

- Spend a few moments acknowledging the power and sovereignty of Almighty God.
- Recognize and repent of any doubt or fear you may have allowed to creep into your thoughts.
- Next, ask the Lord Jesus Christ to make you alert to opportunities around you to become a channel of hope and supernatural help to those around you who are suffering.

PENTECOST IN TOPEKA

Gordon Robertson

"And they were all filled with the Holy Spirit and began to speak with other tongues, as the Spirit gave them utterance."
Acts 2:4 NKJV

In October of 1900, in Topeka, Kansas, a small band of believers led by Charles Parham started Bethel Bible School. The only textbook was the Bible. Their concerted purpose was to learn the Bible, not just in their heads, but to have each thing in the Scriptures wrought out in their hearts.

In December 1900, Parham sent his students to work to diligently search the Scriptures for the Biblical evidence of the baptism in the Holy Spirit. They all came back with the same answer—when the baptism in the Holy Spirit came to the early disciples, the indisputable proof on each occasion was that they spoke with other tongues.

According to Parham, after midnight on January 1, 1901, during a watch-night service, he laid hands upon a student named Agnes N. Ozman: "I had scarcely repeated three dozen sentences when a glory fell upon her, a halo seemed to surround her head and face, and she began speaking in the Chinese language, and was unable to speak English for three days. When she tried to write in English to tell us of her experience, she wrote the Chinese, copies of which we still have in newspapers printed at that time."

Within 10 years, that tiny prayer meeting in Topeka spread out far and wide to start the Azusa Street revival under William J. Seymour and the healing ministries of John G. Lake and F. F. Bosworth. That meeting ultimately gave birth as well to the Assemblies of God, the Church of God, the Church of God in Christ, and the Pentecostal Assemblies of the World. Thousands of missionaries went out and Pentecostal churches sprung up in Canada, Mexico, South America, all over Europe, Africa, the Philippines, China and even Australia.

All of this was accomplished in 10 years without any formal organization and in spite of the obvious limitations on communication and travel at the turn of the century. These people seemed to have no hesitation to leave everything behind to spread the message that God wanted to pour out His Spirit on all flesh, all nations—Jews and Greeks, slaves and free, male and female, rich and poor. They knew that everyone could come and be filled.

WHAT IS THE HOLY SPIRIT SAYING TO ME?

_____

_____

_____

_____

ACTIVATION
- Re-read Acts 2 and imagine you were there to experience the wind and fire of the Holy Spirit for the very first time.
- Ask God to rush into your life in that same way, with that same power today.
- Don't take the Holy Spirit's presence for granted. Honor Him by operating in His power and strength.

FURTHER STUDY
Acts 2:42–47; Luke 18:27; Mark 16:17

THE HARVEST OF PENTECOST...THE BEST IS YET TO COME

Wayne Hilsden

*"But you shall receive power when the Holy Spirit has
come upon you; and you shall be witnesses to
Me in Jerusalem, and in all Judea and Samaria,
and to the end of the earth."*
Acts 1:8 NKJV

Charles Spurgeon was one of the most eloquent preachers
of all time; yet Spurgeon said, "It would be better to speak six
words in the power of the Holy Ghost than to preach seventy
years of sermons without the Spirit." One of the world's greatest evangelists was DL Moody. But Moody said, "There is not
a better evangelist in the world than the Holy Spirit."

Spurgeon and Moody lived prior to the outpouring at Azusa Street. If these men confessed their need for the power of the
Holy Spirit in their ministries, how much more should we, who
claim to be Spirit-filled, be operating in the Spirit's power!

What were Jesus' last words? They weren't "Go and build a
chain of bless-me clubs." No, He gave the Great Commission:
"Go and make disciples." And what else did He say before He
ascended into heaven? He told His followers that before they
go, they should wait. Wait for the promise of the Father—the
baptism with the Holy Spirit. Then you will "receive power
when the Holy Spirit has come upon you; and you shall be
witnesses . . . to the ends of the earth." World harvest and kingdom expansion were the chief purposes of Pentecost.

The picture of the harvest of souls that will be gathered into his Kingdom is not small, but very great indeed. John had a vision in Revelation 7:9 of "a great multitude which no one could number, of all nations, tribes, peoples, and tongues, standing before the throne and before the Lamb, clothed with white robes, with palm branches in their hands."

This promise is not limited to that one day of Pentecost two millennia ago. For Peter said in his sermon that day in Acts 2: "The promise is (not only) unto you and to your children, (but also) to all that are afar off (i.e. both in space and in time)" (JFB Commentary rendition). The promise of the Holy Spirit being poured out upon "ALL flesh" has not yet been fulfilled. The greatest harvest of all time is still ahead of us. The best is yet to come.

WHAT IS THE HOLY SPIRIT SAYING TO ME?

_____

_____

_____

ACTIVATION
- Evaluate how the Great Commission has made an impact on your life. Ask God to show you how you can take new steps in fulfilling Jesus' last mandate to His disciples.
- Read John's account of his vision of heaven in Revelation 7, and ask God to increase your vision for the harvest in our lifetime.
- Walk in the flow of the Spirit moment by moment so that you will not miss a God–ordained opportunity to introduce someone to Jesus.

SPIRIT OF PRAYER AND PROPHECY

Margaret Court

"Pursue love and desire spiritual gifts, but especially that you may prophesy."
1 Corinthians 14:1 NKJV

The Spirit of prayer is also the Spirit of prophecy. We declare divine utterances as the Spirit inspires us. He directs our prayers by putting things into our hearts; then we pray them back to Him. Any word spoken by God will carry out its intended purpose and never return void (Isaiah 55:11)! None of these words will ever fall flat because they are Spirit-birthed. As we meditate on the Scriptures that God has already quickened to us, they become fuel for our prayer life. The Word becomes settled in us and faith begins to grow.

Words alter the spirit realm. John the Baptist said he was "the voice of one crying in the wilderness" preparing the way of the Lord. We cry in the wilderness for our families, our cities and nations, and we are able to alter them through our prayers. Joel 2:11 says, *"The Lord gives voice before His army."* It is time for prophetic declarations—like missiles—to come forth from His Church with the apostolic authority we have been given. God's words will change things!

WHAT IS THE HOLY SPIRIT SAYING TO ME?

_____

_____

_____

_____

_____

_____

ACTIVATION

- Ask for the Spirit and gift of prophecy to be ignited in your heart. Step out in faith and begin to declare the things God is showing you.
- Let the Holy Spirit bring Scripture to your mind, and then pray it back to Him, declaring His promises over yourself and your family.
- Prophesy God's goodness and provision to your future and the future of His Kingdom!

FURTHER STUDY

Ephesians 6:18; Proverbs 25:1; Isaiah 50:4–5; 1 Corinthians 14:1–5

SPEAKING IN TONGUES

Craig Mosgrove

How is it possible that some of us in the Church have re-
duced one of the most glorious experiences of grace in the
Christian life to simply an act of speaking in tongues (glos-
solalia)? I am concerned that the tenets of the Christian and
Pentecostal life have not been transmitted effectively from one
generation to the next.

Spirit-baptism has no bearing on salvation. It is clear in
Scripture that justification (regeneration) is the initial experience of God for the believer (John 3:3–7). Although it is clear
Scripturally that the Holy Spirit indwells the believer at the
point of salvation, the believer has not yet been Spirit-baptized.

There is a definite, subsequent experience beyond salvation called baptism in the Holy Spirit. It relates not to salvation, but rather to service in the Kingdom of God. The believers in Acts 2 were baptized in the Holy Spirit and spoke in
tongues as the Spirit administered the gift. But why was this
needed? Jesus told them in Acts 1:8 that they would receive
this power to witness all over the earth. These believers were
filled with God, baptized in the Holy Spirit for the sake of mission and witness. It is important to note that while tongues is
evidence of Spirit-baptism, witness is essence.

Salvation is participation in the mission and life of God.
But here is the point we often overlook as Pentecostals: you
can't share His life without sharing His missionary passion.
Why does He baptize believers in the Holy Spirit? To enhance
their witness for Him to the unbelieving world!

Should one speak in tongues? Of course. But is tongue speech, itself, actually being baptized with the Holy Spirit? Of course not. It is the product and empirical evidence of a life that has just been set on fire for Christ's mission to the ends of the earth!

Be born again. Hunger and thirst for righteousness. Be baptized with the Holy Spirit. Speak in tongues as the Spirit prays through you. Then share the Gospel of Jesus Christ with everyone around you. Just don't let tongue-speech distract you—it is the evidence of a heart set ablaze for mission.

WHAT IS THE HOLY SPIRIT SAYING TO ME?

_____

_____

_____

_____

_____

_____

ACTIVATION

- Think about how and when you operate in the gift of tongues. Pray in the Spirit right now and let the Holy Spirit commune with your heart.
- Ask God to show you open doors for sharing the Gospel. Identify several people you can visit this week and introduce to Jesus.

SPEAKING WITH ONE VOICE

Lisa Bevere

The dynamic of foreign languages was birthed at the tower of Babel when God scattered a disobedient people who were on the verge of achieving the impossible:

The impossible would have been possible because of two factors: a united people and a shared language. The people's outright disobedience would have been hailed a success. God put an end to their nonsense by confusing the languages and scattering the people to the four corners of the earth.

Our human existence began with one language, and I believe it will end with one language: the language of God-wonder. Scripture tells of the day of Pentecost in Acts, Chapter 2: . . .And at this sound the multitude came together, and they were bewildered, because each one was hearing them speak in his own language.

Multitudes gather when heaven finds voice on earth. When we have something to say, God finds a way for others to hear it. No one was left out. When we speak His words by the power of His Spirit, astonishing things happen. I long for this unified expression of God-wonder. Even more powerful than a common earthly language is the collective power of saying the same thing. On the day of Pentecost the declarations of heaven invaded earth and all who were present knew it.

Our God Most High is triumphant. His glorious love and wondrous mercy know no bounds. I am hungry for something so much more! I believe we are yet again on the threshold of heaven finding a collective voice on earth.

Whether you believe in speaking in tongues or not, a bigger question is on the table. Will we use our words in a way that unites the Church so we can glorify God? Let's declare His flawless works and allow a unifying work of His Spirit to begin! Commitments to unity will not work unless all the participants are aligned with a higher cause. Let's glorify Him.

WHAT IS THE HOLY SPIRIT SAYING TO ME?

_____

_____

_____

_____

_____

_____

ACTIVATION

- Pray for the Holy Spirit to speak words of unity through you.
- Ask the Holy Spirit to direct your path to those who need words of hope.
- Pray the power of God's Spirit will give you a boldness to speak of His mighty works.

BEFORE AND AFTER

Jeff Farmer

You've seen them before. Pictures of huge, overweight people who discovered the perfect diet and then appear in magazines saying, "I lost 163 pounds!" The difference is jaw-dropping. You naturally share their sense of pride and respect their discipline. As a boy I read muscle magazines, determined to be the next Mr. Universe. I was the "before picture"—the skinny kid who dreamed of a barrel chest, biceps larger than my waist, a washboard stomach, and thunderous thighs.

Before and after images still woo us—Extreme Makeover: Home Edition, The Biggest Loser, Debbie Boone's Lifestyle Lift. Their attraction is the compelling contrast between life before and life after. Consider, then, the contrast between the Christian life before and the Christian life after the baptism in the Holy Spirit. Raised in a mainline Protestant denomination, I have lived in both places. The difference is like night and day—like a desert wilderness compared to an oasis garden.

With the glorious Holy Spirit baptism comes an abundance of grace and gifts rarely, or never, accessed by those who have not been filled with the Spirit. The after Christians shall:

- receive power, be witnesses (Acts 1:8)
- speak with other tongues (Acts 2:4)
- prophesy, see visions, dream dreams (Acts 2:17)
- magnify God (Acts 10:46)
- live according to the Spirit (Rom. 8:5)
- put to death the deeds of the body (Rom. 8:13)

- receive gifts of the Spirit (I Cor. 12:4)
- walk in the Spirit (Gal. 5:16)
- be led by the Spirit (Gal. 5:18)

This is the Promise. This is the Gift. Embrace the after!

WHAT IS THE HOLY SPIRIT SAYING TO ME?

_____

_____

_____

_____

_____

_____

ACTIVATION

- Reflect on your life before you received the baptism in the Holy Spirit. Think about the differences in your life after you received the baptism in the Holy Spirit.
- Jump deeper into the well of the Spirit and let Him show you new dimensions of who He is. Listen for His voice and move whenever He moves.
- Ask the Holy Spirit to show you people in your path today who need a touch from Him. Be the person who will reach out and touch them with His love and power!

SINGING TO BRING WATER

Opoku Onyinah

On the way to Canaan, the Lord gave many prophetic pictures of water and rock to the Israelites. The rock represented Christ and water had diverse lessons to teach us. First, the people of Israel drank from the water that came from the rock, symbolizing the pierced Christ. Second, they drank from the water that came from the rock which was spoken to, which represented the risen Christ.

Third, in Numbers 21:16–18, the leaders of Israel sang and used their staffs to dig a well. This well was a picture of the Spirit, who was to be poured out after the glorification of Jesus. Jesus would no longer be there in the form of a rock, but in the form of the Spirit, who would be working as His people came together to sing His praises. Jesus attributed this Scripture to Himself in John 7:37-38: "On the last day, that great day of the feast, Jesus stood and cried out, saying, 'If anyone thirsts, let him come to Me and drink. He who believes in Me, as the Scripture has said, out of his heart will flow rivers of living water.'" Here, Jesus could be referring to this incident of the digging of the well by the leaders of Israel.

Jesus was giving a picture of springs of living water coming out from the souls of His disciples. He wanted them to move out from the rituals of drawing water from Siloam, which was the tradition during the Feast of Tabernacles, to the reality of receiving the Spirit through Him and speaking in tongues. The One to whom the people of Israel drank during the wilderness experience was there in person.

Shall we, His disciples, like the elders of Israel, sing this song: "Spring up, O well, within my soul"? Shall we stir the gifts in us? We must allow the Spirit to gush out from within our souls so that we can sing praises to the glory of the Almighty God! When we obey the Lord, we no longer strike the rock two times, neither do we keep on speaking and speaking; now we shall sing to His glory.

WHAT IS THE HOLY SPIRIT SAYING TO ME?

_____

_____

_____

_____

_____

_____

ACTIVATION

- What song is in your heart today? Sing it out loud to the Lord.
- Bring your difficult situations to the Lord and praise Him for what He is doing in the middle of those circumstances. Sing over those situations, proclaiming the goodness of God and His promises to you.
- Sing a new song of praise from your heart, especially when you least feel like praising.

LIVING IN CONTINUAL SPIRIT BAPTISM

George O. Wood

When praying for the baptism in the Spirit as a young person, I would hear people use Luke 11:9–13 to teach about it—ask, seek, knock. But I misunderstood these verses. I really didn't think the Holy Spirit wanted to have anything to do with me. I felt that I not only had to ask, but I had to beat the door down.

In reality, this passage reminds us that Spirit baptism is not something we ask for once. It should be something we ask for and expect to receive repeatedly. This is why Jesus used the progressive present tense. Go on asking, go on seeking, go on knocking. There is never any time in your life where you should simply come to rest and say, "I've received all the Spirit of God I'll ever need."

We never have enough of God's Spirit. Yes, we have enough to serve God capably today, but we must replenish the supply of His presence in succeeding days. Jesus gave us a pattern to follow—ask, seek and knock. If you're not filled to the level of your need for the Spirit today, then ask, seek and knock. And go on asking, seeking and knocking, until you're full and satisfied for that moment. Then, there will come another moment where you'll need more of the Spirit. It's right to say, "Father, You promised the Spirit. You promised the baptism in the Spirit. I'm here to ask."

Don't treat the baptism in the Spirit as something that happens only once. Exercise the gift. Paul said to Timothy about his ministry in 2 Timothy 1:6, "Stir up the gift of God, which is in thee by the putting on of my hands" (KJV). The New International Version says "fan into flame." The word for "stir up" is a Greek word that represents a hot coal, an ember, a spark. A charcoal fire needs to be fanned into flame. This is the word Paul used. There will be times when we need the wind of the Spirit of God to rekindle a gift for ministry. This is true with the baptism in the Spirit as well. Kindle, rekindle, keep being filled with the Spirit so that this blessed experience is a regular expression of your relationship with Christ.

WHAT IS THE HOLY SPIRIT SAYING TO ME?

_____

_____

_____

_____

_____

_____

ACTIVATION
- By faith, stir up the gift of God inside you as you pray. Hear what the Spirit has to say about you and agree with Him.
- Ask for more of the Holy Spirit to fill you, transform you and flow out of you.

A 21ST CENTURY PENTECOST

Billy Wilson

The outpouring of the Holy Spirit on the Day of Pentecost as recorded in Acts 2 changed the Church, and the Church changed the world. The same has happened since the renewal of Pentecostal experience 100 years ago. Six hundred fourteen million people, or over thirty percent of all adherents to Christianity, are now Spirit Empowered (Charismatic/Pentecostal) according to the most recent Pew Forum survey. Growth rates in this Empowered movement between 1910 and 2010 were nearly four times the growth rate of Christianity and the world's population. Harvey Cox, a Harvard University professor, says that Spirit Empowered Christianity is "the fastest growing Christian movement on earth."

The immediate presence of God is longed for by this generation. As we face world problems and overwhelming human difficulties, God's power will sustain us. Not only can we survive these tumultuous days on planet earth, we can be empowered to help others find the comfort we know in Him.

First Samuel 3 gives an account of Samuel's calling. The high priest Eli was old. His eyes were growing dim and his spiritual perception was dull. The seven–pronged golden candlestick that was meant to burn day and night in the Holy Place of the tabernacle was burning out. The flame on the candlestick needed to be tended or it would go out, resulting in a deep, cold darkness in the place meant for God's presence. Just before the fire burned out—before the candle grew cold, before the flame flickered for the last time—God CALLED! "Samuel, Samuel!" Samuel misperceived the call as coming from Eli, from man. But the call continued until finally Samuel answered God's voice and became a fiery prophet to his generation. The fire continued to burn!

God is calling for a new generation to experience His fire. The candle burns low in many parts of the world and the place meant for blazing passion has become darkened and cold. Samuel, or Johnny, or Sue, or Asmir, or Pablo—God is calling! Awaken to experience His fire and reach the world in the 21st century.

WHAT IS THE HOLY SPIRIT SAYING TO ME?

_____

_____

_____

_____

_____

_____

ACTIVATION
- Pray for awakening across the globe so that the fire will not go out!
- Ask for a renewed passion in your heart for the people and things of God.
- Pray for spiritual ears to be open to God's call, and that many will follow Him.

ACKNOWLEDGMENT

Receive encouragement and inspiration from leaders in the Spirit-empowered movement. It is our prayer that the Empowered21 devotionals will challenge you to seek the power and presence of the living God. The Holy Spirit brings renewal, direction, comfort, help, healing, restoration, and intercession to the Christian life. Daily moments seeking God's spirit will bring transformation to your heart, your work, your family, and your ministry.

We would like to thank Empowered21 for providing this plan. For more information, please visit www.empowered21.com.

NOTES

NOTES

NOTES